D1423305

9030 00007 3310 2

LONDON BOROUGH OF
WANDSWORTH

9030 00007 5210 2

Askews & Holts

J920 CLEO JUNIOR NON-

WW21004369

CLEOPATRA

GREAT LIVES IN GRAPHICS

Button
BOOKS

Cleopatra VII was the last queen of Egypt. She is one of the most famous women in history and there are many myths and legends about her, but how much truth they contain is still a mystery.

A lot of what is known is taken from a book written 100 years after Cleopatra died called *Life of Antony*, by a Greek author called Plutarch. He is thought to be honest and reliable, but the Romans were masters of "fake news", and after Cleo's death they made up stories about how sly and cunning she was. So today it can be tricky to tell what's true and what's not.

There's still loads we don't know. Was she really a great beauty? How did she charm two rulers of Rome? And what about her death – was it suicide or murder?

Read on and see what you think.

CLEO'S COUNTDOWN!

69 BC — Cleopatra VII is born in Alexandria, Egypt

68 BC — Cleo's little sister Arsinoe IV is bo[rn]

54 BC

52 BC — Cleo is co-ruler of Egypt with her dad

51 BC — Cleo's dad dies, she's made Queen with 10-year-old brother Ptolemy XIII

50 BC — Cleo says she's main ruler and stamps her face on all new coins

49 BC — Ptolemy gets angry and kicks her out of Egypt

48 BC — Cleo snea[ks] into Caesar's room roll[ed] in a rug

41 BC — Cleo and Antony meet. Her sister Arsinoe dies

40 BC — Cleo gives birth to twins, Sun and Moon

39 BC — Antony's wife Fulvia dies

38 BC — Antony marries Octavian's sister

37 BC — Cleo marries Antony

36 BC — Cleo gives birth to Ptolemy Philadelphus

34 BC

66 BC Roman general Pompey the Great defeats the pirates

62 BC Cleo's dad, Ptolemy XII, pays Pompey and Caesar to say he's king

61 BC Cleo's little brother Ptolemy XIII is born...

59 BC ...followed by Ptolemy XIV

Caesar invades Britain

55 BC Cleo's dad back in power and he kills Berenice

57 BC Cleo's mum dies and Berenice rules alone

58 BC Egyptians exile Cleo's dad and older sister Berenice IV takes over

47 BC Caesar says Cleo is Queen again. She gives birth to Little Caesar

46 BC Cleo and Little Caesar visit daddy in Rome

43 BC Caesar's son Octavian rules Rome with Marc Antony

44 BC Romans kill Caesar. Cleo rules with Little Caesar

45 BC Caesar creates new calendar

MONDAY XIV

Antony gives land to his and Cleo's kids at Donations of Alexandria

32 BC Rome gets angry, Octavian declares war on Cleo

31 BC The Battle of Actium

30 BC Antony and Cleo commit suicide

ALEXANDRIA

LIGHTHOUSE

TEMPLE OF ISIS

GREAT HARBOUR

ROYAL HARBOUR

CANOPIAN GATE

GYMNASIUM

PHAROS

EUNOSTOS HARBOUR

LIBRARY

CANAL

MOON GATE

SERAPEUM

1000M

ALEXANDER THE GREAT

Cleo was born in Alexandria, Egypt in 69BC. The city was founded by Greek ruler Alexander the Great back in 331BC when he conquered Egypt. After Alexander's death one of his generals – Ptolemy I – took over and declared Alexandria the capital. He turned it into the biggest, most cosmopolitan city on the planet. It boasted a 30-metre-wide main avenue, shining limestone colonnades, the largest library on Earth, palaces on the harbour and a monumental lighthouse.

RLAND!

PHAROS LIGHTHOUSE

One of the seven wonders of the Ancient world, the Lighthouse of Alexandria was one of the first ever built. It was constructed on the tiny island of Pharos to help guide ships into Alexandria's busy harbour, and it was the world's tallest building at the time, aside from the Great Pyramid of Giza.

BUILT: 290BC

It took 20 years to build! Many slaves lost their lives

137 METRES HIGH

In Egyptian money this was around 800 "talents"

COST: £2.5 MILLION

TODAY'S TALLEST!

828M	508M	452M	443M
Burj Khalifa	Taipei 101	Petronas Towers	Sears Tower

DESTROYED: 1480

Earthquakes in 956, 1303 and 1323 badly damaged the lighthouse

FAMILY FEUDS!

When Cleo was born her family had ruled Egypt for nearly 300 years. Known as the Ptolemaic Dynasty, they weren't actually Egyptian, but Greek, and as families go, they were one of the most ferocious in history. When they weren't trying to kill each other or seize the throne, they were marrying one another instead.

PTOLEMY IV

Murdered his mum, married his sister

PTOLEMY V

Had his mother's murderers killed

PTOLEMY VI

Fought his brother, married sister Cleopatra II

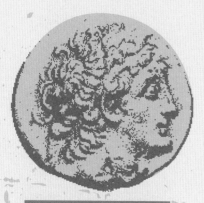

PTOLEMY X

Killed his mother (Cleopatra III), married his niece (Berenice III)

PTOLEMY XI

Also married Berenice III, who was his sister or mother, but had her killed after 19 days!

PTOLEMY XII

Kicked out of Egypt by his daughter Berenice IV, then killed her

MURDER

 MARRIED

 FIGHT

 MURDERED BY

TO MAKE LIFE SIMPLE (OR MORE CONFUSING) ALL BOYS IN THE PTOLEMAIC DYNASTY WERE NAMED PTOLEMY (PRONOUNCED TOL-UH-MEE) AND GIRLS WERE CALLED CLEOPATRA, BERENICE OR ARSINOE — CLEOPATRA WAS ACTUALLY THE SEVENTH ONE IN HER FAMILY!

PTOLEMY VII

Murdered by his uncle (Ptolemy VIII) at a wedding feast or may have been murdered by his father (Ptolemy VI)

PTOLEMY VIII

Probably murdered Ptolemy VII, married Cleopatra II. Murdered his son

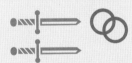

PTOLEMY IX

Tried to kill his mother (Cleopatra III), married both sisters, fought his brother (Ptolemy X)

By all accounts Cleopatra was as ruthless as the male members of her family!

BERENICE IV

Probably killed her sister (Arsinoe IV), killed her husband

CLEOPATRA VII

Married and fought her brother (Ptolemy XIII), married and probably killed her other brother (Ptolemy XIV)

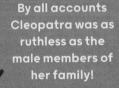

CLEVER CLEO!

Cleo was probably much smarter than most people think. A teen queen, she'd already ruled with her father for four years by the time she came to the throne at 18, and history suggests she was a wise politician.

SPENT CHILDHOOD STUDYING:

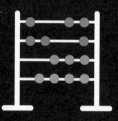

MATHS

LITERATURE

PHILOSOPHY

WROTE BOOKS ABOUT:

 **MEDICINE**

SCIENCE

DID YOU KNOW!

She was the first of her Greek family to learn Egyptian, and spoke eight other languages

Cleo styled herself as the new Isis, one of the most important goddesses of ancient Egypt, so that her people would like her

FAMOUS POLYGLOTS

languages

39

ITALIAN CARDINAL
GIUSEPPE MEZZOFANTI

58

LIBERIAN
ZIAD FAZAH

DID YOU KNOW?

A person who can speak several languages is called a

POLYGLOT

CHILD PRODIGY **WILLIAM JAMES SIDIS** SPOKE 8 LANGUAGES BY THE AGE OF 8!

100

BRITISH ECONOMIST
SIR JOHN BOWRING

200

FRENCH PHILOLOGIST
GEORGES DUMÉZIL

OH BROTHER!

When Cleo was 18, her dad died. He left Cleo and her 10-year-old brother Ptolemy XIII in charge, expecting them to rule Egypt together. In those days it was normal for pharaohs to marry their sisters, so the two of them got hitched. But it certainly wasn't a case of happily ever after . . .

ROMAN NUMERALS

Today historians use Roman numbers to label kings and queens of the past so they know which one is which. Cleo's little brother was Ptolemy XIII. That's the same as saying he was Ptolemy the 13th.

Here's how it works:

The Romans put letters together to make bigger numbers.

$$XIII = 13$$
$$X = 10 \quad I = 1$$
$$X + I + I + I$$
$$= 13$$

50BC

Cleo was determined to be Egypt's main ruler, and had her face stamped on all new coins

50BC

Ptolemy wasn't happy that Cleo was taking over, so he and his advisors plotted against her

JULIUS CAESAR

49BC

Meanwhile, two of Rome's greatest generals, Julius Caesar and Pompey the Great, were also in the middle of a civil war

49BC

Ptolemy's power grew. He forced Cleo to flee to Syria and made himself sole pharaoh

SYRIA

EGYPT

48BC

Hoping to impress Caesar, Ptolemy pretended to be friends with Pompey, before chopping off his head

48BC

Ptolemy presented Caesar with Pompey's head, but Caesar wasn't happy – turns out Pompey was also Caesar's son-in-law, oops!

POMPEY THE (NOT SO) GREAT

M
1000
D
500
C
100
L
50
X
10
V
5
I
1

Romancing ROME!

Cleo knew that if she was to beat her brother Ptolemy and become a powerful Egyptian queen, she needed legendary Roman general Julius Caesar on her side. So when she heard that Caesar was in Alexandria, she decided to try and win him over.

1 ROLL UP, ROLL UP!

Legend has it, to get past her brother's guards, Cleo snuck into the palace hidden inside a rolled-up rug. When Caesar saw her, he was captivated

2 DEATH ON THE NILE

Caesar tried to persuade Ptolemy to let Cleopatra come back as co-ruler, but Ptolemy wasn't keen. He and his advisors fought Caesar in a battle and Ptolemy ended up drowning in the river Nile

4 BAD BLOOD

Cleo took Little Caesar to visit his dad in Rome, but the people of Rome weren't happy about it – Caesar already had a Roman wife, and they were worried he might try to make Alexandria the new Roman capital

3 LOVE CHILD

Caesar made Cleopatra queen again. Together they had a son called Ptolemy Caesar, who they nicknamed "Caesarion", meaning "Little Caesar"

5 ON THE RUN

On 15 March, 44BC, a group of 60 Roman senators stabbed Caesar 23 times. Cleo was forced to flee back to Egypt. With Caesar dead, two new men took over – Roman general Marc Antony and Caesar's adopted son and heir, Octavian

DID YOU KNOW?

Caesar was once kidnapped by pirates. While held captive he joked he would return one day and kill them. After he escaped, he had them caught and executed

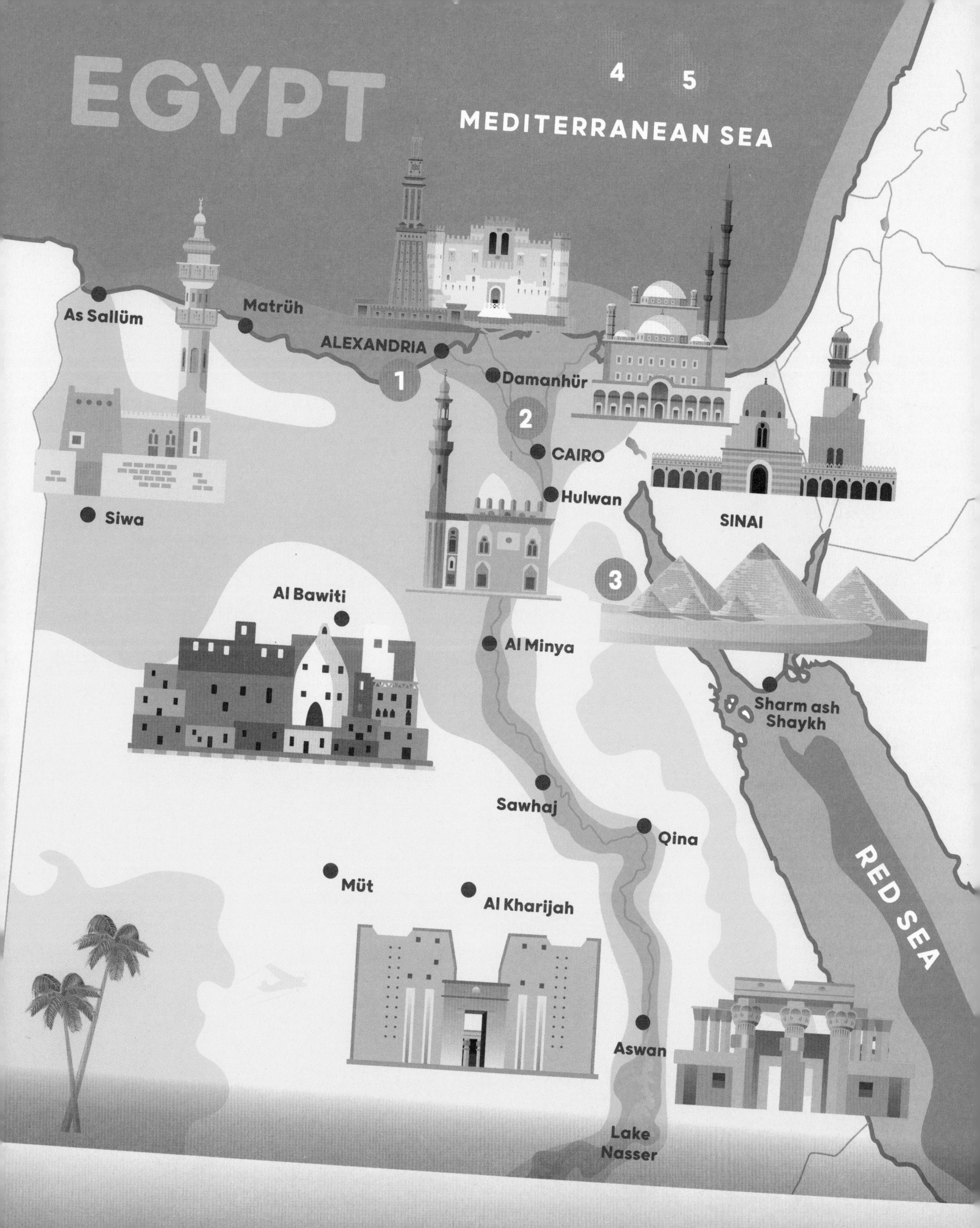

EGYPT

4 5

MEDITERRANEAN SEA

As Sallüm

Matrüh

ALEXANDRIA

1

Damanhür

2

CAIRO

Hulwan

SINAI

Siwa

Al Bawiti

3

Al Minya

Sharm ash
Shaykh

Sawhaj

Qina

RED SEA

Müt

Al Kharijah

Aswan

Lake
Nasser

FIRST DATE

Julius Caesar got the idea for a leap year from the Egyptians and created a new Roman calendar which is the basis for the one we use today. Cleo's family also introduced star signs to the Egyptians. A famous Egyptian carving of the zodiac was found on the ceiling of one of their temples. We still don't know what all the signs and symbols mean, but we can have fun guessing . . .

THE NILE
THE BEGINNING

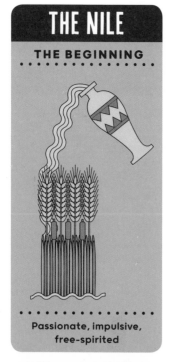

Passionate, impulsive, free-spirited

AMUN
GOD OF CREATION

Optimistic, intuitive, inspirational

MUT
CONSORT OF AMUN

Practical, determined, unromantic

GEB
GOD OF EARTH

Diplomatic, tactful, sensitive

ANUBIS
GOD OF MUMMIFICATION

Introverted, solitary, emotional

SETH
GOD OF CHAOS

Ambitious, rebellious, hot-tempered

BASTET
CAT GODDESS OF PLEASURE

Alluring, charismatic, successful

SEKHMET
LIONESS GODDESS OF WAR

Perfectionist, proud, stoical

OSIRIS
GOD OF THE UNDERWORLD

Adaptable, moody, easy-going

ISIS
GODDESS OF MAGIC AND WISDOM

Loving, lucky, energetic

THOTH
GOD OF KNOWLEDGE

Hard-working, thoughtful, patient

HORUS
GOD OF THE SKY AND STARS

Creative, industrious, responsible

WHAT'S YOUR STAR SIGN?

JANUARY
1 2 3 4 5 6 7
8 9 10 11 12 13 14
15 16 17 18 19 20 21
22 23 24 25 26 27 28
29 30 31

FEBRUARY
1 2 3 4 5 6 7
8 9 10 11 12 13 14
15 16 17 18 19 20 21
22 23 24 25 26 27 28
29

MARCH
1 2 3 4 5 6 7
8 9 10 11 12 13 14
15 16 17 18 19 20 21
22 23 24 25 26 27 28
29 30 31

APRIL
1 2 3 4 5 6 7
8 9 10 11 12 13 14
15 16 17 18 19 20 21
22 23 24 25 26 27 28
29 30

MAY
1 2 3 4 5 6 7
8 9 10 11 12 13 14
15 16 17 18 19 20 21
22 23 24 25 26 27 28
29 30 31

JUNE
1 2 3 4 5 6 7
8 9 10 11 12 13 14
15 16 17 18 19 20 21
22 23 24 25 26 27 28
29 30

JULY
1 2 3 4 5 6 7
8 9 10 11 12 13 14
15 16 17 18 19 20 21
22 23 24 25 26 27 28
29 30 31

AUGUST
1 2 3 4 5 6 7
8 9 10 11 12 13 14
15 16 17 18 19 20 21
22 23 24 25 26 27 28
29 30 31

SEPTEMBER
1 2 3 4 5 6 7
8 9 10 11 12 13 14
15 16 17 18 19 20 21
22 23 24 25 26 27 28
29 30

OCTOBER
1 2 3 4 5 6 7
8 9 10 11 12 13 14
15 16 17 18 19 20 21
22 23 24 25 26 27 28
29 30 31

NOVEMBER
1 2 3 4 5 6 7
8 9 10 11 12 13 14
15 16 17 18 19 20 21
22 23 24 25 26 27 28
29 30

DECEMBER
1 2 3 4 5 6 7
8 9 10 11 12 13 14
15 16 17 18 19 20 21
22 23 24 25 26 27 28
29 30 31

DID YOU KNOW?

The Egyptian calendar used **12 MONTHS** of only **30 DAYS.** They added **5 DAYS** of festivals at the end to add up to **365!**

ANTONY & CLEOPATRA

Caesar's death meant Cleo needed a new Roman ally, and she set her sights on Roman general Marc Antony. Egypt was fabulously wealthy but needed protecting from invasion. Rome had a huge army, but needed money to fight wars. So Cleo gave Antony money, and Antony protected Egypt. It was a match made in heaven . . .

WHERE DID THEY MEET?

TURKEY

In Tarsus, a city in modern-day Turkey

WHAT WERE THEIR PASTIMES?

HUNTING

FISHING

DRINKING

GAMES

FEASTING

WHAT DID CLEO DO TO IMPRESS HIM?

She sailed up the Cydnus River in a golden barge with perfumed purple sails and silver oars. Attendants dressed as cupids played flutes and fanned her as she relaxed under a gilded canopy

This painting by Sir Lawrence Alma-Tadema shows Cleo sailing into Tarsus

WHY IS THEIR RELATIONSHIP SO FAMOUS?

In around 1623 William Shakespeare wrote a play about them.

Since then Cleopatra has been the subject of at least:

5 BALLETS **45** OPERAS **77** PLAYS **7** FILMS

"Friends, Romans, countrymen, lend me your ears"

Antony and Cleo dreamt of creating a great empire in the East

Legend has it that after a night of feasting Cleo and Antony would dress up as slaves and go into the city, knocking on doors and playing tricks on people

DID YOU KNOW?

Antony once had a job where he had to work out what might happen in the future by watching birds fly. This was a hugely important role in Roman times!

HOW MANY CHILDREN DID THEY HAVE?

3

Twins Alexander Helios and Cleopatra Selene, and a son called (you guessed it) Ptolemy

The twin's last names mean "sun" and "moon"

CLEOPATRA'S
Beauty Secrets

Cleo's beauty is legendary. Roman historian Cassius Dio said she was "a woman of surpassing beauty" who was "brilliant to look upon". But she's actually the faceless queen – no one really knows what she looked like. Her face does appear on ancient coins, where she looks hook-nosed and manly, but this could have been done on purpose to intimidate her enemies. Whether she was gorgeous or not, we do know the Egyptians were one of the first civilisations to use perfumes, oils and other beauty treatments.

The milk from **700** donkeys

Eyebrows were painted black using burnt almonds

30 DAYS
to create the material for kohl eyeliners

3
CASTOR SESAME MORINGA
oils used on the face to combat wrinkles and preserve youth

10% GREASE
probably goose fat, was found in cosmetic powders recovered from the tombs of pharaohs

16
ingredients in kyphi, a famous Egyptian perfume produced from berries, honey, flowers and wine

"Her beauty, as we are told, was in itself not altogether incomparable, nor such as to strike those who saw her"

Plutarch, Greek historian

for one **milk bath**

No one knows what Cleopatra looked like!

Did you know?

For the Egyptians, makeup was useful as well as beautiful. Kohl (a dark powder used as eyeliner) was said to have anti-bacterial properties and to keep out the sun's glare, while kyphi (an Egyptian perfume) may have been used as a medicine for liver and lung ailments

Girl with a pearl

Cleopatra

Instructions

1. Take very expensive pearl
2. Drop it into vinegar
3. Wait until it dissolves
4. Drink it!*

Very expensive pearl

Pearl value:

£23.5m

(10m sestertii)

Vinegar

By today's standards, Cleopatra was super rich. Egypt was a wealthy country thanks to industries like glass, wheat and papyrus, and Cleo pocketed all the profits. She used the cash to show off to Rome, betting Marc Antony she could hold the most expensive dinner party ever. Legend has it she put on a fabulous banquet, and while Antony was enjoying the feast she grabbed a gigantic pearl from a pair of her earrings, dropped it into a goblet of vinegar, let it dissolve and then swallowed the lot.

Goblet

Did you know?

Scientists have worked out that white vinegar would take more than a day to dissolve a pearl weighing about one gram. The calcium carbonate in a pearl reacts with the acetic acid in vinegar to produce calcium acetate – water and carbon dioxide. So Cleo may have accidentally invented fizzy water!

*Don't try this at home

There were obviously no photographs of this incredibly costly incident but Italian artist Giambattista Tiepolo painted what it might have looked like in 1744!

Other famous gemstones

Bahia Emerald
1.7m carats

Guinness Emerald
1,759 carats

Chaiyo Ruby
109,000 carats

Star of Adam Sapphire
1,404 carats

Letseng Diamond
910 carats

£200-760m
£410m
£370m
£80-250m
£40-80m

Cleo made roughly 12,500 talents a year. That could have bought around:

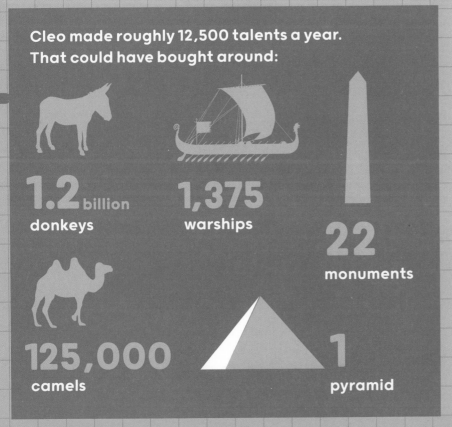

1.2 billion
donkeys

1,375
warships

22
monuments

125,000
camels

1
pyramid

SPOILT ROTTEN!

Antony and Cleopatra were determined their kids would rule the world one day, and invited the whole city of Alexandria to a spectacular celebration, where they divided up Rome's lands between them and told everyone Cleo's oldest son, Little Caesar, was the heir to Rome. The kids couldn't believe their luck.

KEY ⭕ = 1 YEAR
Age when became King or Queen

⬤ What they got

DID YOU KNOW?

Caesar's other son and heir, Octavian, ruled the western part of Rome's lands. He was so angry when he heard that Antony and Cleo had said Little Caesar was the heir to Rome, he declared war on Cleopatra

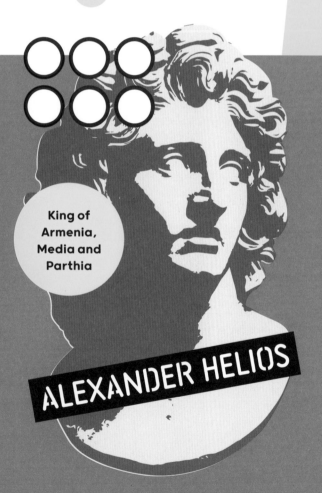

ALEXANDER HELIOS

King of Armenia, Media and Parthia

CLEOPATRA SELENE II

Queen of Cyrenaica and Libya

PARENTS: CLEOPATRA & ANTONY

KEY

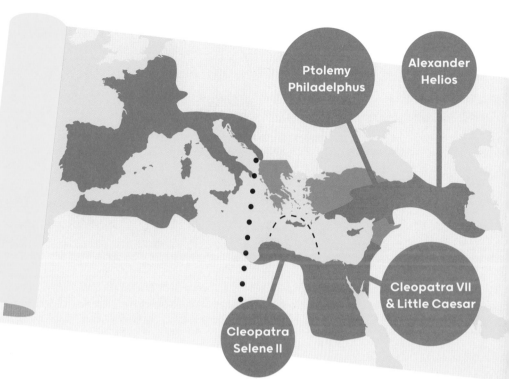

- Roman provinces belonging to Antony
- Italy and Roman provinces belonging to Octavian
- Territories given to Cleopatra's children
- • • • Boundary between Antony and Octavian

Ptolemy Philadelphus

Alexander Helios

Cleopatra VII & Little Caesar

Cleopatra Selene II

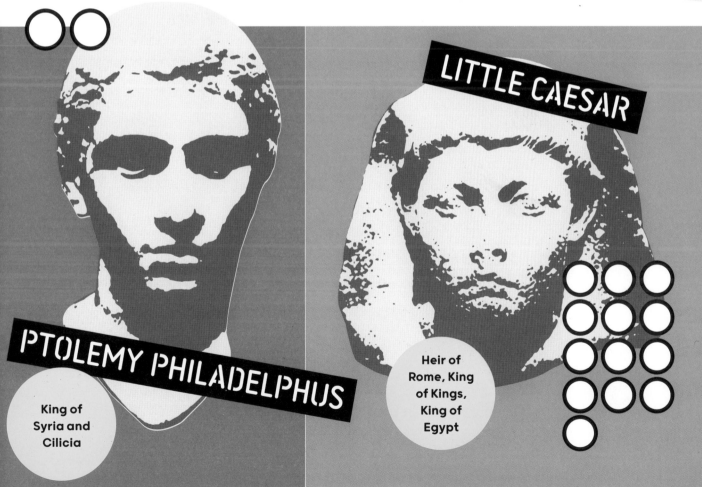

PTOLEMY PHILADELPHUS

King of Syria and Cilicia

LITTLE CAESAR

Heir of Rome, King of Kings, King of Egypt

PARENTS: CLEOPATRA & CAESAR

CLASH
OF THE
TITANS!

Caesar's other son, Octavian, was so angry when he heard that Antony and Cleo had said Little Caesar was the heir to Rome, he declared war on them. The two armies met in a tremendous sea fight called the Battle of Actium. It raged all morning until Cleopatra, worried they were losing, turned and fled the scene, taking her ships with her. Antony managed to escape, but most of his fleet was burnt or sunk and Octavian was declared master of the Roman world.

One way of stopping the massive Roman warships was to break their oars, leaving them stranded

Antony's fleet was largely made up of giant Roman warships called deceres, loaded with enormous stone-throwing catapults and battering rams

OARSOME!

3 **LAYERS OF ROWERS**

DECERES

2-6 **CATAPULTS**

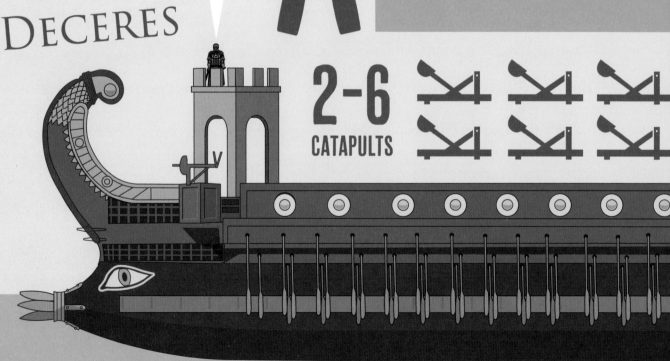

LIBURNIAN

Octavian's ships were smaller Liburnians, but this made them easier to manoeuvre

33 METRES

BATTERING RAM

Warships were often fitted with wooden battering rams strengthened with bronze. These could smash a hole in the side of an enemy ship and sink it

10-15 SAILORS

15-30

40 MARINES

200-250

144 ROWERS

572 ROWERS

BALLISTA

Huge catapults and a machine called a ballista launched stones and bolts at enemy ships, breaking and splintering masts and decks

2 FIGHTING TOWERS

DID YOU KNOW?

Even in calm waters lots of sailors and soldiers drowned, because hardly any knew how to swim

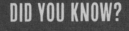

44 METRES

SUICIDE BY SNAKE

Cleopatra's death is shrouded in mystery. She and Antony fled to Egypt after the Battle of Actium. When Octavian's army reached Alexandria, Antony bravely rode to the battlefield to face him, but hearing false news that Cleo had been killed, he fell on his sword. Discovering she was still alive, Antony then had himself carried to her side, where he died. Overcome with grief, Cleo is said to have committed suicide. How she did this still isn't clear, though. Stories say an asp – probably an Egyptian cobra – bit her on the arm.

ALTERNATIVELY...

Greek historian Plutarch says she also hid deadly poison in her hair combs

Cleopatra was only **39** when she died, and she had been queen of Egypt for **21** years

DID YOU KNOW?

Cleopatra may have tortured prisoners by testing poisons on them

WHAT HAPPENED NEXT?

Octavian took over after Antony and Cleo died, and the Roman Empire was born

Today there are still lots of deadly snakes around the world. Look how many people the venom from these snakes could kill in just a single bite . . .

INLAND TAIPAN

BLACK MAMBA

30

SAW-SCALED VIPER

6

KING COBRA

11

EASTERN BROWN SNAKE

58

289

DEATH OF A DYNASTY

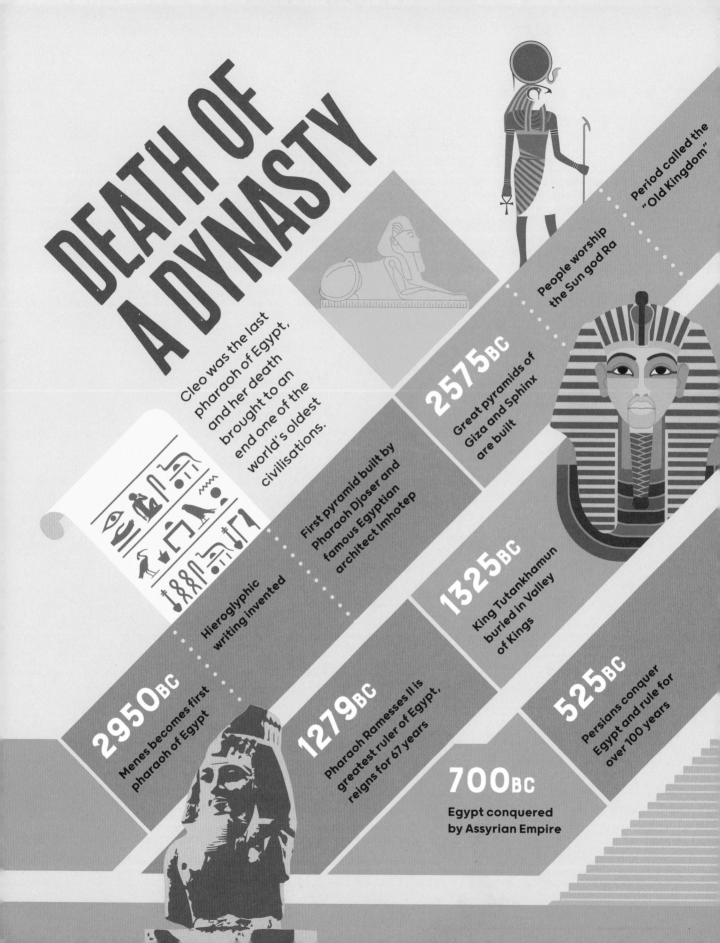

Cleo was the last pharaoh of Egypt, and her death brought to an end one of the world's oldest civilisations.

Period called the "Old Kingdom"

People worship the Sun god Ra

2575BC
Great pyramids of Giza and Sphinx are built

First pyramid built by Pharaoh Djoser and famous Egyptian architect Imhotep

Hieroglyphic writing invented

1325BC
King Tutankhamun buried in Valley of Kings

2950BC
Menes becomes first pharaoh of Egypt

1279BC
Pharaoh Ramesses II is greatest ruler of Egypt, reigns for 67 years

700BC
Egypt conquered by Assyrian Empire

525BC
Persians conquer Egypt and rule for over 100 years

The civilisation lasted

3,000
years

DID YOU KNOW?

Cleopatra lived closer to the creation of the iPhone than she did to the building of the Great Pyramid. The Great Pyramid was built around 2560BC, while Cleopatra lived around 69-30BC. The iPhone was launched in 2007, which is about 500 years closer

1975BC
Pharaoh Mentuhotep II rules over the "Middle Kingdom"

Irrigation is used for the first time, carrying water from the Nile to crops

1640BC
Horse and chariot introduced

1520BC
Start of the "New Kingdom"

Pharaoh Amenhotep III builds Temple of Luxor

332BC
Alexander the Great conquers Egypt and builds Alexandria

Pharaoh Tuthmosis I is first tomb in Valley of Kings

Hatshepsut is successful female pharaoh, rules for 22 years

305BC
Ptolemy I is pharaoh and Ptolemaic dynasty begins

30BC
Last pharaoh, Cleopatra VII Thea Philopator, dies

GLOSSARY

CIVILISATION
A well-organised society that cares about science, art and culture

CIVIL WAR
A war between groups of people in the same country

CO-RULER
A person who rules together with someone else

DECERES
A huge ancient warship

DYNASTY
A family that rules over a country for a long period of time

EMPIRE
A group of countries or areas that are ruled over by a single leader or government

HARBOUR
A place on the coast that's sheltered so that ships can anchor there safely

HEIR
The person who will inherit someone's crown, title, money or possessions after their death

HIEROGLYPHICS
The ancient Egyptian alphabet

HISTORIAN
A person who studies or writes about history

KOHL
A type of black makeup that is often used to line the eyes

LEAP YEAR
A year with one extra day on 29 February. A leap year occurs every four years

LIBURNIAN
A small galley ship used by the Roman navy

MYTH
An idea or story that is believed by many people but isn't true

PHARAOH
A ruler of ancient Egypt

POLYGLOT
Someone who knows several languages

SENATE
The group of people (or senators) who made the laws in Rome

SESTERTIUS
An ancient Roman coin

TALENT
An ancient unit of weight, usually in gold or silver

ZODIAC
An imaginary band in the sky that the sun, moon and planets appear to travel through

Button Books

First published 2020 by Button Books, an imprint of Guild of Master Craftsman Publications Ltd, Castle Place, 166 High Street, Lewes, East Sussex, BN7 1XU, UK. Copyright in the Work © GMC Publications Ltd, 2020. ISBN 978 1 78708 059 1. Distributed by Publishers Group West in the United States. All rights reserved. No part of this publication may be reproduced, stored in a retrieval system or transmitted in any form or by any means without the prior permission of the publisher and copyright owner. While every effort has been made to obtain permission from the copyright holders for all material used in this book, the publishers will be pleased to hear from anyone who has not been appropriately acknowledged and to make the correction in future reprints. The publishers and authors can accept no legal responsibility for any consequences arising from the application of information, advice or instructions given in this publication. A catalogue record for this book is available from the British Library. Senior Project Editor: Susie Duff. Design: Matt Carr, Jo Chapman. Illustrations: Matt Carr, Shutterstock, iStock, Alamy. Colour origination by GMC Reprographics. Printed and bound in China.